Getting More Out of Lent

SOMETHING MORE FAITH SERIES

By Deacon Keith Strohm

Mark Hart, Series Editor

the WORD
among us®
Press

Published by The Word Among Us Press
7115 Guilford Drive, Suite 100
Frederick, Maryland 21704

23 22 21 20 19   1 2 3 4 5

ISBN: 978-1-59325-348-6

Nihil Obstat: Msgr. Michael Morgan, J.D., J.C.L.
Censor Librorum
November 19, 2018

Imprimatur: +Most Rev. Felipe J. Estévez, S.T.D.
Diocese of St. Augustine
November 19, 2018

Cover design by Suzanne Earl

Made and printed in the United States of America

Contents

What Are You Waiting for?

By Mark Hart
Something More Series Editor

When you ask most Catholics about Lent, they'll probably tell you that we're not supposed to eat meat on Fridays or that we're supposed to give up foods and drinks that we love. You might even hear that we're not supposed to say the "A" word at Mass (you know, the one that rhymes with "shmalleluia"). Obviously, though, if that's all there was to Lent, the Church wouldn't go to so much trouble encouraging us to make bigger changes in our lives.

Lent is more than just a season before Easter during which we give things up. Lent is a forty-day journey for our mind, body, and soul. On that journey, as Deacon Keith Strohm explains, we take time to think about how we've turned away from God. We think of our sins and of how we've hurt others. And we repent. But the journey isn't only about repenting; it's also about forgiveness and healing and receiving God's unstoppable mercy. We're not alone on that Lenten journey, Deacon Keith points out—God is with us every step of the way.

Turning and Returning

Repenting is an action. It's deciding to go 180 degrees in the other direction. It's like a spiritual U-turn. One of the prayers you might hear on Ash Wednesday as the ashes are placed on your forehead is "Turn away from sin, and return to the gospel" (see Mark 1:15).

The first action of repentance, the "turning away from sin," is a ninety-degree movement to the right. We're no longer trapped by sin. But turning ninety degrees only leaves us better off, not free. It's in the *next* ninety degrees—when we "return to the gospel"—that we go for the win. It's in this movement that we forsake the lies and the false securities of sin and find the healing love of God—the Father welcoming back his prodigal child, the Savior who wants to unbind us and set us free. It's in that return to the gospel that we find the heart of Lent and God's magnificent love that lights up our whole existence.

Of course, during Lent we are challenged to make sacrifices in our lives, and Deacon Keith offers suggestions to get us started. But his suggestions and this booklet have one goal: to help us receive God's healing love and never-ending mercy.

Get Ready for New Life

So what are you waiting for?

This Lent, prepare to receive the freedom and the new life Jesus died to give you.

I pray that this booklet will help you get more out of Lent—more love, more joy, more peace.

Say a prayer, now, asking the Holy Spirit for the grace you need to make the most out of this season of Lent, giving the Spirit permission to lead you even more deeply into the heart of God and the life of Christ's Church on earth. God bless you on this journey!

How to Use This Booklet

Whether used individually or in a small group, each session of *Getting More Out of Lent* is designed to take under an hour. If you use it on your own, remember to begin and end each session with prayer. You might also want to find someone to talk to about what you're learning.

If you are part of a small group, the following guidelines can help you have a fruitful experience:

1. Establish a prayerful environment by taking time to pray before beginning. Ask the Holy Spirit to be with your group. Pray "Come, Holy Spirit" slowly several times. Allow for a few moments of silence. Then say a prayer together, like the Our Father or Hail Mary or Glory Be.

2. Assume everyone has read the commentary beforehand. The group facilitator can ask everyone if this is the case. If it is not, you might ask one or two people to summarize the main points or say what most struck them from the reading.

3. Discuss the questions, being careful not to rush to the next one, especially if not everyone has spoken. Some people need more time to gather their thoughts. Some may need a moment of silence before they feel free to express themselves.

4. If the discussion strays, try to bring it back to the questions or the text. Any member of the group should feel free to gently steer the discussion to the next point.

5. When you are finished with the questions, the group facilitator should outline the Lenten Resolution section at the end and ask whether anyone has any questions about it. Encourage participants to do the suggested Lenten resolution.

6. End with prayer. Perhaps someone could pray spontaneously, thanking God for the opportunity to gather together to pray and study God's word.

7. Make sure you know when and where you are gathering for the next session. Participants will get the most out of each small group session if they read the Scripture passage and commentary and reflect on the questions before the group gathers again.

GET THE MOST OUT OF YOUR BOOKLET

Before each session, visit **wau.org/faithseries** for a short video from the author.

SESSION ONE

You are Deeply Known and Loved

John 4:5-26

So he came to a town of Samaria called Sychar, near the plot of land that Jacob had given to his son Joseph. Jacob's well was there. Jesus, tired from his journey, sat down there at the well. It was about noon.

A woman of Samaria came to draw water. Jesus said to her, "Give me a drink." His disciples had gone into the town to buy food. The Samaritan woman said to him, "How can you, a Jew, ask me, a Samaritan woman, for a drink?" (For Jews use nothing in common with Samaritans.) Jesus answered and said to her, "If you knew the gift of God and who is saying to you, 'Give me a drink,' you would have asked him and he would have given you living water." [The woman] said to him, "Sir, you do not even have a bucket and the well is deep; where then can you get this living water? Are you greater than our father Jacob, who gave us this well and drank from it himself with his children and his flocks?" Jesus answered and said to her, "Everyone who drinks this water will be thirsty again; but whoever drinks the water

I shall give will never thirst; the water I shall give will become in him a spring of water welling up to eternal life." The woman said to him, "Sir, give me this water, so that I may not be thirsty or have to keep coming here to draw water."

Jesus said to her, "Go call your husband and come back." The woman answered and said to him, "I do not have a husband." Jesus answered her, "You are right in saying, 'I do not have a husband.' For you have had five husbands, and the one you have now is not your husband. What you have said is true." The woman said to him, "Sir, I can see that you are a prophet. Our ancestors worshiped on this mountain; but you people say that the place to worship is in Jerusalem." Jesus said to her, "Believe me, woman, the hour is coming when you will worship the Father neither on this mountain nor in Jerusalem. You people worship what you do not understand; we worship what we understand, because salvation is from the Jews. But the hour is coming, and is now here, when true worshipers will worship the Father in Spirit and truth; and indeed the Father seeks such people to worship him. God is Spirit, and those who worship him must worship in Spirit and truth." The woman said to him, "I know that the Messiah is coming, the one called the Anointed; when he comes, he will tell us everything." Jesus said to her, "I am he, the one who is speaking with you."

I remember my first day of junior high school as if it were yesterday.

Stepping through the doorway of an unfamiliar building, I was immediately awash in a sea of chaos. Shouting, laughter, and the press of students and faculty quickly overwhelmed me. I had spent six years in a much smaller, very nurturing grade school environment, where everyone knew me. Now I was practically a number—unknown and unloved in a sweeping press of strangers. I remember feeling alone and afraid as I searched for my new homeroom class.

> The Lord . . . awaits you there, wherever your particular well might be located.

Have you ever experienced something similar? Have you felt overwhelmed by the pace of life or by the challenges and obstacles life brings? Maybe things have been slowly falling apart at work, among your friends, or in your family. Maybe trying to care for everybody else's needs has been weighing you down or making you feel as if you and your own needs are invisible. Maybe things are going well in your life, but in the midst of the beautiful relationships you have, God seems distant and aloof—more like a theory than a loving presence by your side. Maybe you're carrying around guilt or shame because of something that you have done, or because of something that's been done to you, and you feel isolated and alone.

The Samaritan woman in the passage above might have felt some of these same things. Her relationships made her the talk of the village—she'd had five previous husbands, and currently she was with a man to whom she wasn't married! No wonder she went to the well at noon, one of the hottest parts of the day, when she could be sure no one else would be around. She was criticized, looked down on, and largely separated from the community.

And yet, it is to her that Jesus goes, tired from his own journey, and asks for a drink of water. In the course of their conversation, she comes to understand that he is not simply a man, but the Messiah, the anointed one of God, who sees her, who knows her, and yet who does not condemn her. It is in this encounter with the Lord that the Samaritan woman understands that she is not the sum of her failures, sins, and brokenness but that she is one who is beloved by God.

The Well of Encounter

The truth is that we all have times and seasons when we feel as though we are at a well in the heat of the day—a little lost, or alone and unloved. We all have those moments when we wonder if anyone is really listening or really understands what we are going through. As you begin this Lenten journey, the Lord invites you to know the One who created you, who knows and loves you, and who awaits you there, wherever your particular well might be located.

You are not an afterthought or a random assortment of molecules. You were made in the image and likeness of God (see Genesis 1:26). The Father intentionally brought you into being and gave you life for a purpose, and this God, in Jesus, sustains you every single moment. Paul, writing about Jesus to the Colossians, says that "he is before all things, and in him all things hold together" (1:17).

Well, what does that really mean?

It means that not only did God create you out of nothingness and call you into being, but also that every heartbeat and breath you draw in this life, as well as every "moment" of life in eternity, is an intentional choice made by the God who is gazing upon you, who knows everything about you, and who delights in you because you are his.

Remember that story I shared about starting in a new school? I recall that day so clearly—not only because of the pain, anxiety, and loneliness I experienced, but also because one teacher saw my fear and came over to me. He asked me my name, told me everything was going to be okay, and walked me to my homeroom. Because of his kindness and willingness to enter into my life, he transformed that first day of school and helped set the stage for the rest of my time in junior high.

Sometimes we are so focused on the repentance and mortification elements of Lent that we miss out on something fundamental—that the purpose of Lent is to prepare us for Easter, for an experience of freedom and new life in Jesus Christ. Jesus knows and loves us, as he knew and loved the Samaritan woman—deeply and completely. He knows what is going on in our lives, what troubles us, and what makes us joyful. He draws close to us and wants to enter our brokenness—to transform us and quench our deepest thirst with his living water.

He is simply waiting for our response.

1. What are some areas in your life where you feel over-whelmed, lost, alone, or as if no one is able to see you or understand what you are going through?

2. What would it take for you to invite Jesus into those places? In other words, what is keeping you from asking Jesus to give you living water in those areas?

3. If you asked the Lord to describe how he felt about you in one word, what do you think he would say?

4. Do you have someone in your life who truly knows you? How did that relationship begin, and what impact has it had on your life?

5. If you knew, without a shadow of a doubt, that God loved you fully and completely, not for what you did (or do), but for who you are, how do you think that would change your life?

Lenten Resolution

Prayer is one of the central ways that we deepen our relationship with God. Make the commitment this week to spend at least fifteen minutes a day talking to God and telling him what's going on in your heart. Take several minutes to sit and listen to God to see if he has anything to say to you. Feel free to ask him specific questions, and wait to see if you sense him answering you. If it helps, write down anything that you hear.

Some parishes have regular times of Adoration, when you can sit silently before the Lord present in the Eucharist. Try to spend time at least once this week in Adoration, perhaps pondering that one word that reveals what God feels about you (see question 3).

SESSION TWO

God's Word Has Power for Your Life

Matthew 4:1-11

Then Jesus was led by the Spirit into the desert to be tempted by the devil. He fasted for forty days and forty nights, and afterwards he was hungry. The tempter approached and said to him, "If you are the Son of God, command that these stones become loaves of bread." He said in reply, "It is written:

'One does not live by bread alone,
but by every word that comes forth from the mouth of God.'"

Then the devil took him to the holy city, and made him stand on the parapet of the temple, and said to him, "If you are the Son of God, throw yourself down. For it is written:

'He will command his angels concerning you'
and 'with their hands they will support you,
lest you dash your foot against a stone.'"

Jesus answered him, "Again it is written, 'You shall not put the Lord, your God, to the test.'" Then the devil took him up to a very high mountain, and showed him all the kingdoms of the world in their magnificence, and he said to him, "All these I shall give to you, if you will prostrate yourself and worship me." At this, Jesus said to him, "Get away, Satan! It is written:

'The Lord, your God, shall you worship
and him alone shall you serve.'"

Then the devil left him and, behold, angels came and ministered to him.

Our culture is saturated with messages.

We are bombarded by commercials, marketing pitches, pleas for our attention, the latest diet fads and popular self-help approaches to life—all of them coming at us through billboards, magazines, televisions, computers, tablets, and even our phones. In such an environment, it's easy to become distracted or confused about what is most important in life or to forget what is most important about each of us as individuals created and loved by God. What can make us happy? Is it the latest technological gadget or time spent binge-watching Netflix? Could a better paying job or a nicer car bring us the fulfillment we have been searching for? What is the source of our dignity and value? Is it the amount of weight that we've lost, or the number of people on our social media friends list?

Jesus understands this confusion. When he withdrew into the desert to pray, he was assailed by the enemy, who tried to lead him away from his mission with conflicting messages and lies. The Son of God responded to each temptation in the desert with a quote from Scripture—specifically a quote from the Old Testament Book of

Deuteronomy, which chronicled the Israelites' own temptations to turn away from God as they wandered in the desert for forty years.

Why did he respond with Scripture?

Because Jesus understood that the Old Testament Scriptures were not simply a collection of historical books, poems, and other literary genres but, rather, one of the ways in which God reveals who he is and who his people are—their deepest identity. He understood the power of God's word. The temptations the Israelites experienced were the same temptations that Jesus experienced in the desert and that we experience—to put worldly concerns first, and trust in God and fidelity to him second. Jesus put these temptations behind him and affirmed his identity as God's faithful Son when he used Scripture to stand firm.

> God himself speaks to us in Scripture.

Jesus demonstrates that more than just a historical artifact or a collection of "dead" letters, the Bible is a "two-edged sword," as the author of the Letter to the Hebrews says (4:12), a source of wisdom and power. "In Sacred Scripture," the *Catechism of the Catholic Church* states, "the Church constantly finds her nourishment and her strength, for she welcomes it not as a human word, 'but as what it really is, the word of God.' 'In the sacred books, the Father who is in heaven comes lovingly to meet his children, and talks with them'" (104). In short, God himself speaks to us in Scripture.

Isn't that amazing? Not only do we encounter Jesus in the sacramental life of the Church, but God also comes to meet us when we enter prayerfully into the Scriptures. The full passage in the Letter to the Hebrews puts it this way: "Indeed, the word of God is living and effective, sharper than any two-edged sword, penetrating even between soul and spirit, joints and marrow, and able to discern reflections and thoughts of the heart" (4:12). Through the power of the Holy Spirit, we encounter the risen and living Jesus in a personal way when we read the Bible, and Jesus reveals the Father. God wants to meet us, speak to us, instruct us, console us, challenge us, and transform us in and through our reading of Scripture *every single day.*

That might seem a little overwhelming to you. If you grew up Catholic, you may have a vague sense that you're not supposed to read the Bible, or maybe someone discouraged you from picking it up. Or you may have had a large, coffee-table Bible in your home that seemed too ornamental or unwieldy to take up and read. Or perhaps the Bible just seems difficult to understand, and you're too uncomfortable to even try. Don't let that apprehension or past experience stop you from exploring God's word in Scripture. You don't need a degree in biblical studies or a theology degree to start praying with the Bible and listening to the Lord as he speaks to you. You just need an open heart and the discipline to spend regular time with the Bible.

Imagine that. God speaking with you! We believe that when the Scriptures are proclaimed at Mass, it is the Lord who is speaking in the midst of our faith community in this time and in this place. However, we have a much harder time imagining that he would want to speak with us and reveal his love for us individually, in our prayer time, as we read the Bible. But this Word became flesh just for you and me, and he longs to speak with you. Come to meet him in the pages of the Bible, and allow him to share with you the truth of his love for you!

1. What was your earliest encounter with the stories from the Bible? Did you read the Bible at all growing up? Did anyone read the stories from the Bible to you?

2. Do you have a favorite story or passage from the Bible? What is it, and why is it so important to you?

3. Do you believe that the Bible can help you with the circumstances and situations of your life today? Why or why not?

4. Is it easy or difficult for you to read and pray with the Bible? Why?

5. Name one thing that keeps you from reading the Bible regularly. What would it take to remove or work around that obstacle in your life?

Lenten Resolution

If you don't already do so, add some Scripture reading to your daily prayer time beginning this week. You might want to start with Mark's Gospel, since it is the shortest of the four Gospels. If you find it difficult to pray with the Bible, try entering into the story using your imagination. Use a daily devotional such as *The Word Among Us*, or find a website or app that offers audio files of the Bible. As the narrator reads the Scripture passage, imagine that you are present in that story. Pay attention to the sights and sounds—what are you smelling, hearing, and seeing? Who are you in that story? Are you a bystander, a follower of Jesus, one of the apostles? As you imagine yourself in the story, how are you reacting interiorly to what is happening there? When we engage the Bible in this way, we are doing more than just reading; we are allowing the words of Scripture to penetrate our thoughts, will, and emotions more deeply.

As you begin your time of Scripture reading, ask the Lord to help you become receptive to his word and give you the grace to understand both the truth of what you are reading and how best to put it into practice. Throughout this Lenten journey, your desire to read Scripture will grow and, with it, your responsiveness to the action of the Holy Spirit in the pages of the Bible.

SESSION THREE

God Wants to Heal You and Set You Free

John 5:1-9

After this, there was a feast of the Jews, and Jesus went up to Jerusalem. Now there is in Jerusalem at the Sheep [Gate] a pool called in Hebrew Bethesda, with five porticoes. In these lay a large number of ill, blind, lame, and crippled. One man was there who had been ill for thirty-eight years. When Jesus saw him lying there and knew that he had been ill for a long time, he said to him, "Do you want to be well?" The sick man answered him, "Sir, I have no one to put me into the pool when the water is stirred up; while I am on my way, someone else gets down there before me." Jesus said to him, "Rise, take up your mat, and walk." Immediately the man became well, took up his mat, and walked.

The stories of Jesus in the Bible include many instances of healing, and it's easy to conclude that they are simply tales made up to teach a truth about him. The Gospels are not fiction, however; they are narratives that detail the life, ministry, death, and resurrection of Jesus. If we see the Gospels as fictional stories, it becomes a simple matter to dismiss the things that Jesus and his disciples did. All too easily we can slip into the habit of viewing the healings of Jesus as metaphors for his goodness.

For sure, Jesus is good, but many of the people he met needed the healing of their whole person, body and soul. And that was the mission of Jesus! We call that mission one of salvation. The Greek word from which we derive the word "salvation" is *sozo*, which holds multiple meanings, including to "heal," "protect," "save," and "deliver." So in a very real sense, Jesus came not only to save us from sin and restore us to a relationship with the Father, but also to bring healing, restoration, and deliverance to our bodies, souls, and the entire created order.

We know that the Jesus whom we worship is the same Jesus who walked the earth two thousand years ago, and his mission of healing and salvation has not ended. In fact, the *Catechism* states that:

> Christ's compassion toward the sick and his many healings of every kind of infirmity are a resplendent sign that "God has visited his people" and that the Kingdom of God is close at hand. Jesus has the power not only to heal, but also to forgive sins; he has come to heal the whole man, soul and body; he is the physician the sick have need of. His compassion toward all who suffer goes so far that he identifies himself with them: "I was sick and you visited me." His preferential love for the sick has not ceased through the centuries. (1503)

The question we should ask ourselves on this journey through Lent is not "Does God heal?" but rather "What is it within me that needs the healing touch of God?" We may not feel as if we deserve this healing because of what we have done or what has been done to us, but the truth is that Jesus does not weigh our sins against our good works before he offers healing and wholeness. Rather, he is asking us the very same question that he asked the man at Bethesda: "Do you want to be well?"

God doesn't always heal us in the way we want, and it may seem that no one understands the issues we deal with, or the difficulties we go through. But the Lord does not abandon us in our suffering, struggles, illness, or brokenness. Rather, he has chosen to remain with us in the midst of those sufferings, and he offers us the very life of God's kingdom to bring us freedom and healing.

What is it within me that needs the healing touch of God?

Sometimes, he will transform our hearts, and this can change our whole experience of suffering. This happened in my own life. I was born with a below-elbow amputation—I'm missing my right hand. Experiencing that disability shaped my life, and not always in a positive way. Growing up, I had a great deal of anger and bitterness, toward myself and God—until I encountered the love of the Father in Jesus Christ through the power of his Holy Spirit. After that encounter, my whole experience of living with a disability shifted and changed. My disability remains, but my brokenness and pain have been transformed.

Healing is essential to Jesus' mission. In the Gospel of John, Jesus says, "I came so that they might have life and have it more abundantly" (10:10). Remember that when Jesus raised his friend Lazarus from the dead, he instructed those who surrounded the now-living Lazarus to "untie him" so that he would be free of the burial cloth (John 11:44). Just as Jesus desired that Lazarus would live unbound, he also desires that you would live in freedom. He wants to free you from your fears, addictions, anxieties, shame, unforgiveness—anything that holds you back from fully serving him and enjoying the abundant life that he offers you.

As you enter this week of Lent, let this be the center of your reflection: Jesus has given his life for you. Do you truly want to be well?

Questions for Reflection and Discussion

1. Do you know someone who is suffering in mind or body? How can you help them "rise" and encounter the love of Jesus?

2. What do Jesus' healings say about his identity? What does his desire to bring you to healing say about your identity?

3. What do the words "healing" and "freedom" mean to you? What are the areas in your life that are in most need of healing and freedom?

4. The man at the pool of Bethesda couldn't move fast enough to get into the pool to receive healing. What obstacles do you think exist in your life that keep you from receiving the freedom that God desires for you?

Spend time this week praying the Stations of the Cross, meditating on the suffering of Christ. Ask him to reveal to you the areas in your life that he died to set free. Bring those areas to God in prayer each day, and ask for the grace to release them to him. As you do that, you can pray in these words (or something similar):

"Heavenly Father, I ask that you would take these specific wounds [name them] and unite them to the wounds of your Son, Jesus, on the cross. As I release them to you, fill me now with the freedom and life of your kingdom. I thank you, Father, for the work of grace within me that is bringing me to life and freedom. Grant me the courage to cooperate with what you are bringing to birth in my life. Amen."

Couple this week's Lenten resolution with fasting to intensify your prayer. Give up something that you enjoy doing or fast from a meal.

SESSION FOUR

God Is Waiting to Forgive You

Luke 15:11-32

Then he said, "A man had two sons, and the younger son said to his father, 'Father, give me the share of your estate that should come to me.' So the father divided the property between them. After a few days, the younger son collected all his belongings and set off to a distant country where he squandered his inheritance on a life of dissipation. When he had freely spent everything, a severe famine struck that country, and he found himself in dire need.

So he hired himself out to one of the local citizens who sent him to his farm to tend the swine. And he longed to eat his fill of the pods on which the swine fed, but nobody gave him any. Coming to his senses he thought, 'How many of my father's hired workers have more than enough food to eat, but here am I, dying from hunger. I shall get up and go to my father and I shall say to him, "Father, I have sinned against heaven and against you. I no longer deserve to be called your son; treat me as you would treat one of your hired workers."'"

So he got up and went back to his father. While he was still a long way off, his father caught sight of him, and was filled with compassion. He ran to his son, embraced him and kissed him. His son said to him, 'Father, I have sinned against heaven and against you; I no longer deserve to be called your son.'

But his father ordered his servants, 'Quickly bring the finest robe and put it on him; put a ring on his finger and sandals on his feet. Take the fattened calf and slaughter it. Then let us celebrate with a feast, because this son of mine was dead, and has come to life again; he was lost, and has been found.' Then the celebration began.

Now the older son had been out in the field and, on his way back, as he neared the house, he heard the sound of music and dancing. He called one of the servants and asked what this might mean. The servant said to him, 'Your brother has returned and your father has slaughtered the fattened calf because he has him back safe and sound.' He became angry, and when he refused to enter the house, his father came out and pleaded with him.

He said to his father in reply, 'Look, all these years I served you and not once did I disobey your orders; yet you never gave me even a young goat to feast on with my friends. But when your son returns who swallowed up your property with prostitutes, for him you slaughter the fattened calf.' He said to him, 'My son, you are here with me always; everything I have is yours. But now we must celebrate and rejoice, because your brother was dead and has come to life again; he was lost and has been found.'"

Let's be honest. Our relationship with the Father is often wounded or incomplete in some way, perhaps tied up with experiences we have had with our earthly parents. Sometimes we struggle with the image of the Father as a taciturn, angry, and judgmental presence, one whose love for us depends on our ability to live as perfectly as we can. Or maybe we believe the Father is distant, removed from the details of everyday life, so majestic that he isn't concerned with the particulars of anyone's life, let alone ours.

> From the moment you turned away from the Father, he has been searching for you.

The Father, of course, knows that these are the ways we think of and see him. So he sent his Son, Jesus, to reveal the truth about his heart. Reflect on that for a moment. The Father cares about us enough to send Jesus to dwell with us and, through the sacraments, to dwell within us, demonstrating the depth of the Father's love for us.

That reality reveals not only something about the Father, but also something about who we are in the Father's eyes—beloved children. Sin, of course, breaks our relationship with God. When we sin, we are choosing to reject the Father's love, his place in our life, and our identity in him. But as Jesus makes clear in the Gospel passage above, it is not God who moves away from us when we sin—we move away from him.

However, there is a danger whenever we encounter a Bible story that we have heard many times. Our familiarity can close us off to the message the Lord wants to share with us. The parable of the prodigal son is, perhaps, one of the best-known of Jesus' parables—it is also one of the most radical . . . and the one whose message we frequently overlook.

What do I mean?

At the heart of this parable is a father who is actively searching for his son. If the father were not searching for the son, he would have been be unable to see him "while he was still a long way off" (Luke 15:20). The same is true of your heavenly Father. It doesn't matter what you have done, or how deep your sin goes. From the moment you turned away from the Father, he has been searching for you, calling out your name and awaiting your return.

Yes. It's true.

The Father is waiting to forgive you.

The prodigal son returned to his father's house out of an imperfect, and—let's be clear—rather selfish motive (he was starving), yet he received the father's forgiveness. Like the prodigal son, you too are cherished by the Father you may have spurned, and he longs to embrace you and celebrate your return. Looking closely at the father's reaction, we see that he doesn't focus on his son's repentance or even talk about consequences the son must face for treating him so poorly. Rather, he moves to restoration and rejoicing.

Sometime, guilt can keep us from returning to the Father. But guilt can operate as a positive experience if we see it as a movement of the Holy Spirit in our conscience and our heart, alerting us that we have wandered off the right path. In many ways, guilt can be an invitation from the Holy Spirit to return to the heart of the Father's love.

But there is another experience that seems similar to guilt, though with none of its potential fruitfulness. That experience is shame. Guilt says, "I have made a mistake," but shame has a different message: "I *am* a mistake." If we move into a place of shame, we very quickly start to believe that we are what we have done wrong. We believe that by our very nature, we are outside the scope of the Father's love—beyond his forgiveness and restoration.

But the Scriptures are clear—"There is no condemnation for those who are in Christ Jesus" (Romans 8:1). Jesus took upon himself the sins of the world and ransomed us from the power of shame, darkness, and death. The Father sees our sins, an, when we turn to him with contrition, he welcomes us by name; for he knows that our identity doesn't rest on what we have done. It rests only on his love for us—which is unfailing!

You are not your history or the sum of the sins you have committed. You have an identity as son or daughter. You have a place in the Father's heart and a name that can never be taken from you because it is inscribed on the very hands of God (see Isaiah 49:16).

You are loved. No matter where you are . . . welcome home!

Questions for Reflection and Discussion

1. What do you think of when you hear the word "mercy"? How would you describe the mercy of God? Can you give an example?

2. Have you ever had an experience where you received forgiveness from someone else? What was it like for you to receive that forgiveness?

3. Have you ever forgiven someone else who hurt you, betrayed you, or broke a relationship with you? What did it feel like to offer that forgiveness?

4. How often do you seek the forgiveness of the Lord in the Sacrament of Reconciliation? If infrequently, what do you think keeps you from celebrating that sacrament on a more regular basis?

Lenten Resolution

Many parishes offer additional times for Confession during Lent. Schedule a time to receive the Sacrament of Reconciliation and keep that appointment. Before you go, ask the Lord in prayer to reveal those places and times when you have broken your relationship with him since your last confession. You might find it helpful to prayerfully walk through the Ten Commandments in order to make a fruitful examination of conscience.

After you confess, thank God for his mercy, and consciously envision yourself releasing those sins to the Lord. Ask for the grace also to release the guilt associated with those sins.

SESSION FIVE

Jesus Died to Give You Life

John 3:16-21

For God so loved the world that he gave his only Son, so that everyone who believes in him might not perish but might have eternal life. For God did not send his Son into the world to condemn the world, but that the world might be saved through him. Whoever believes in him will not be condemned, but whoever does not believe has already been condemned, because he has not believed in the name of the only Son of God.

And this is the verdict, that the light came into the world, but people preferred darkness to light, because their works were evil. For everyone who does wicked things hates the light and does not come toward the light, so that his works might not be exposed. But whoever lives the truth comes to the light, so that his works may be clearly seen as done in God.

You are a son or a daughter designed for communion with God and eternal life with him.

This was God's plan when he created our first parents, Adam and Eve. God created humanity not out of a lack of something, such as an unmet desire or a need for companionship. Rather, he called us into being out of an abundance of love—because that's his nature. Love always seeks after the beloved; love always goes outside of itself.

When we look to God himself, we see that the love of God is so powerful and infinite that the Father, Son, and Holy Spirit are present to one another in an eternal exchange of unlimited love. This is the dynamic of love. It is creative, it is self-giving, and it is designed to be freely given away. And we were created to experience and share in this love, here and now and in the life to come. God created us for intimacy, wholeness, and communion.

Sin, however, has separated us from that destiny. Adam and Eve abused their free will and turned away from God, and the stain of this original sin spread throughout all of creation. Cut off from the source of the One who is life, human beings are now subject to illness, suffering, and death.

But Love has stepped in, unwilling to leave us in our sin. The Father sent his Son, Jesus, to call us back to the fullness of life. When Jesus says, "I came so that they might have life and have it more abundantly" (John 10:10), the word that the Gospel uses for "life" is a Greek word, *zoe*. That word, *zoe*, means a particular kind of life. It has multiple meanings, including fullest life and perfect life—in other words, divine life.

Out of love for us Jesus chooses to take upon himself the brokenness and sins of the world, and to suffer and die, so that we can live freely in the abundant life of the resurrection.

Let's make this more personal!

There are things that you have struggled with throughout your life: burdens that you carry because of your brokenness and the sinfulness of others, events that have scarred you. There are lies that you have come to believe about who you are and what you might deserve in this life. Fear, self-hatred, anger, shame, bitterness, abandonment, disappointment—all the hallmarks of life in this world, some of which you may have taken upon yourself. All of these things are the result of the Fall and the wounding of God's creation. They exist because we have been separated from the source of life itself.

Yet Jesus, knowing and seeing you, freely chose to embrace suffering and death so that you could live in freedom, not held back by brokenness or the chains of dysfunction. The life that Jesus lived while he was on the earth and that he lives now in eternity is the life for which you were created. He wants you to begin to experience that life—and its peace, patience, gentleness, self-control, joy, fulfillment, mercy, forgiveness—not at some unspecified time in the "next life," but beginning here and now.

> **We were created to experience and share in this love, here and now and in the life to come.**

What would it mean for you—personally, every day— if fear no longer ruled you, or if the voice of accusation no longer drove you? What would it mean if the burdens you carry in this life could be transformed by the person, the presence, and the power of Jesus Christ and the life he offers you?

The beautiful thing is that you don't have to earn this life. It doesn't depend on your goodness or perfection. It is a free gift and it comes from God when you surrender your heart to him. When you do, then every day offers the opportunity to grow more and more like this Jesus who gave his life for you. Are you ready to begin living that life now?

1. What does it mean to you that Jesus died to give you life?

2. Have you ever had an experience of the full life to which Jesus invites you? When and in what way?

3. Have you given your life in some measure in order that someone else might be able to live or live better? What was that experience like for you?

4. Can you imagine how your life might be different if you lived fully the life that Jesus offers you? What would it look like? What would it feel like?

5. What might be keeping you from receiving this newness of life today?

Lenten Resolution

Make a firm decision to prayerfully accompany Jesus through his passion during the Easter Triduum (Holy Thursday, Good Friday, Holy Saturday) by attending each of these liturgies. While there, ask the Lord specifically why he would choose to go through that experience for you? As the Church enters the sacred season of Easter, write down specific ways that you will live out the new life of the kingdom that you have received in Jesus. How will you continue the spiritual practices that you adopted this Lent?

In preparation, make a list of all of the areas in your life where you want or absolutely need the full and restorative life of Jesus Christ. As you pray through the Triduum, see yourself specifically inviting Jesus into those places. Say to him, "I surrender this to you, my Lord."

Getting More Out of Prayer
by Patricia Mitchell

Prayer is where we meet with God and grow in a relationship with him. Deepen your connection with the Lord through weekly reflections and prayer exercises.

Getting More Out of Mass
by Fr. John Muir

Sometimes life's cares, hard-to-understand readings, and even not-so-great music can distract us from what Jesus wants to give us in the Mass. Fr. John Muir provides reflections to help you get the most out of Mass.

Getting More Out of Confession
by Joel Stepanek

Experience the Sacrament of Reconciliation as an encounter with love and mercy itself. In this booklet, Joel Stepanek invites you to welcome Jesus, the Divine Physician, to heal your heart.

GET THE MOST OUT OF YOUR BOOKLET

Before each session, visit **wau.org/faithseries** for a short video from the author.